New Muslims

ZIYO PIROV

CONTENTS

INVITING NON-MUSLIMS TO THE RIGHT PATH: DELIVER THE MESSAGE IN THE BEST WAY POSSIBLE

Objectives:

·   To understand the role of a person who calls others to the path of Islam.

Arabic Terms:

·   Shariah - Islamic Law

·   Rabb - literally means, lord, owner, master, or leader. Islamically it is mostly used to refer to Allah - the Owner, the Master, the One who takes care of, sustains, nourishes, and takes care of everything.

·   Dawah - sometimes spelt Da'wah. It means to call or invite others to Islam.

·   Insha'Allah – God willing, if God wills it to be so. It is a reminder and acknowledgment that nothing happens except by the will of Allah.

The thing about knowing the truth, understanding the purpose of life and knowing the answer to that age old question of why am I here, is that it is exciting; jumping out of your skin exciting. Thus, on discovery, the first thing you want to do is tell other people, and sometimes just blurting out one of life's universal truths can be a little bit confronting. Some might think you are crazy or deluded, but that is not the problem, because that puts you in such noble company as Prophet Muhammad or Prophet Noah. The problem is that when we invite people to the truth of Islam, we want them to listen and understand just what it is we are trying to say. Therefore, for the benefit of those jumping out of their skin we will discuss a few tips for inviting others to the right path.

First off let us get our definitions in sync. The verb, invite, means to request the presence or participation of in a kindly, courteous, or complimentary way.[1] Shariah literally means 'a path to water,' the source of all life, thus Islamically Shariah is the straight path to Allah, the Giver and Originator of all life. Allah tells us to:

"Invite (call) to the way of your Rabb with wisdom and beautiful preaching and argue with them in a way that is better..." (Qur'an 16:125)

Whenever we invite a person to Islam, to the right path, we are presenting them with the attractions and allurements of Islam. Our job is to deliver the message in the best way possible according to our knowledge and abilities. Acceptance or rejection of the message is up to the person concerned; there is no compulsion in religion and moreover it is Allah who bestows guidance. We are not converting or reverting them because it is Allah, and Allah only that truly does that. Our role is only to assist others on their journey or to plant a seed that will one day, Insha'Allah, grow into a tree of Islam.

"Let there be no compulsion in religion. Truth has been made clear from error…" (Quran 2:256)

"…Say, 'To Allah belongs the east and the west. He guides whom He wills to a straight path.'" (Quran 2:142)

It is important to remember however that conveying the message and calling people to Islam or giving dawah, as many like to call it, is an obligation upon all Muslims. Of course, we are not all expected to work in the field of dawah but we are expected to be aware at all times that our behavior, words and actions, are dawah. Those not familiar with Islam look to Muslims to see just what this religion is all about. Prophet Muhammad said, "Convey from me, even if it is one verse".[2] Quran also reiterates the same message.

"… And who is better in speech than one who invites to Allah and does righteousness and says, 'Indeed, I am of the Muslims.'" (Quran 41:33)

It all sounds very easy, doesn't it? We all love Allah and His Messenger Muhammad and without a doubt we hope that all people will one day feel the same way. However, love for Islam and all it entails is not quite enough. When one accepts the challenge to convey the message one needs to be prepared. No longer can we scowl at the shopkeeper when prices rise. No longer can we react with anger when somebody mumbles an insult as we walk by. A person delivering the message of Islam must be prepared to accept insults, be patient, make sacrifices, and listen to ideas and ideologies that are far from the truth of Islam. Prophet Muhammad said that, "The believer who mixes with people and bears their insults with patience is better than the one who does not mix with people or bear their insults with patience." [3]

Anyone who is recognizably Muslim is conveying the message every time they appear in public or mix with non-believers, therefore our words should always be kind and gentle, and our temper must be completely under control so that harsh words never leave our mouths. One of Prophet Muhammad's companions said, "We smile at people even if in our hearts we are cursing their words or behavior".[4] Moreover a Muslim makes things easy for others. This is what Allah expects and Prophet Muhammad encouraged when he said, "Teach and make things easy, do not make them difficult. If any of you becomes angry, let him keep silent." [5]

"... Allah intends for you ease, and He does not want to make things difficult for you..." (Quran 2:185)

Prophet Muhammad understood human weaknesses and at the same time understood human potential for excellence. His dawah methods were perfect; we have only to follow his example to be sure that we fulfill our obligation to convey the message far and wide. He always chose the easier option for himself and others. However, he made sure that the easier option was within the framework of the shariah.

In the next lesson we will look more carefully at ways to spread the message.

INVITING NON-MUSLIMS TO THE RIGHT PATH: TAWHEED FIRST

Objectives:

· To understand that Tawheed is the basis of Islam and thus the foundation stone of dawah.

Arabic Terms:

· Tawheed - The Oneness and Uniqueness of Allah with respect to His Lordship, His Names and Attributes and in His right to be worshipped.

· Sahabah - the plural form of "Sahabi," which translates to Companions. A sahabi, as the word is commonly used today, is someone who saw Prophet Muhammad, believed in him and died as a Muslim.

· Surah – chapter of the Quran.

· Sunnah - The word Sunnah has several meanings depending on the area of study however the meaning is generally accepted to be, whatever was reported that the Prophet said, did, or approved.

▪   Dawah - sometimes spelt Da'wah. It means to call or invite others to Islam.

▪   Deen - the way of life based on Islamic revelation; the sum total of a Muslim's faith and practice. Deen is often used to mean faith, or the religion of Islam.

When explaining the message of Islam, the most important thing to remember is Tawheed. It must form the basis of any explanation we give about any topic related to the deen. Tawheed is the basis of Islam and without a doubt our discussions must emanate from this important principle.

Quran emphasizes that every messenger sent by Allah began by inviting his people to Tawheed.

"And We sent a messenger to every nation (proclaiming): 'Worship Allah and shun false deities!'..." (Quran 16:36)

"And We never sent any messenger before you, except that we revealed to him that 'There is no deity worthy of worship except Me, so worship Me' "(Quran 21:25)

"Indeed, We sent Noah to his people, and he said, 'O my people! Worship Allah! You have no other deity other than Him. Certainly, I fear for you the torment of a Great Day!'" (Quran 7:59)

According to learned people both past and present, any call to Islam that does not begin with Tawheed is doomed to failure. Prophet Muhammad instructed the sahabah to preach Tawheed when sending them to various communities. To those who went to Yemen he said, "You are going to the People of the Book, so let the first thing that you invite them to be the Tawheed of Allah".[1]

The title 'People of the Book' refers to the Jews and the Christians, those given scriptures for guidance before the Quran was revealed. It is often easier to start a conversation about Islam with Christians and Jews because they already believe in God. Quran is filled with references, and stories that can be easily related to and to which they already have their own versions. For instance, mentioning the surahs of Quran that are named after easily recognizable people such as surah 19 – Maryam (Mary), surah 14 - Ibrahim (Abraham) or surah 12 – Yusuf (Joseph).

Quran beseeches Prophet Muhammad to call the People of the Book to Islam. And Prophet Muhammad in his Sunnah made clear the relationship between all of the prophets and messengers of Allah.

"Say O Muhammad 'O people of the Scripture (Jews and Christians): Come to a word that is just between us and you, that we worship none but God (Alone), and that we associate no partners with Him, and that none of us shall take others as lords besides God.'" (Quran 3:64)

"And argue not with the People of the Scripture unless it be in (a way) that is better, save with such of them as do wrong; and say, 'We believe in that which has been revealed unto us and revealed unto you; our God and your God is One, and to Him we have submitted'". (Quran 29:46)

"I am the nearest of all the people to the son of Mary, and all the prophets are brothers and there is none between me and him (i.e. there is no other prophet between me and Jesus)." [2]

"If a man believes in Jesus and then believes in me, he will get double reward." [3]

People who have no understanding of any of the three monotheistic religions, such as Buddhists require different guidelines. It is the responsibility of the person giving dawah to have a basic understanding of the beliefs of the non-believers they are calling to. Buddhism for instance is a way of life, but not in the same sense as Islam. Put simply Buddhism, as well as many eastern religions have a concept by which the person who does good actions will eventually attain Godlike qualities. On the other hand, Hindus believe in one Supreme God among many, and some of the more obscure religions such as Zoroastrianism and Baha'i do include the concept of One Supreme God. However, you do not want to speak down to anyone as if you know more about their belief system then they do themselves. This is important whether that is the case or not. Remember, you do not want to offend anybody or inadvertently start an argument. More information about other religious beliefs can be found on our other website www.islamreligion.com.

If a person has a strong belief in God or even a nameless Supreme Being responsible for the creation, it is possible to teach them that the God we call Allah is the same God that they call by other names such as Elohim or Yahweh. However, at the same the time it is important to clarify to them that we consider Him to be Alone without any partners and we do not give any of His attributes to creation. We believe that there is a clear line between the Creator and the creation and everything besides God Himself, is His creation.

It is imperative for people to understand that the religion of Islam was revealed for all of humankind, not just one ethnic group or race. Often people want to know the purpose of their lives and Islam gives an unambiguous answer to this question. We have been created to recognize God and worship Him alone, that is, to obey Him in all matters.

"And I did not create the jinn and mankind except that they should worship Me." (Quran 51:56)

One who believes in any sort of God is a theist but those who do not, are called atheists. The two beliefs are polar opposites; atheists do not believe in any supreme being of any description. They do however believe that the world is a better place if governed by man-made ideologies such as capitalism or communism. Thus, there is no ideological common ground from which to begin a discussion about the religion of Islam. Try to remember that the starting point and the basis of dawah is calling a person to belief in One God – Allah. Just as Prophet Muhammad did, we start with the call to Tawheed and we do so by appealing to reason.

We are able to clearly observe and thus point out that everything in the universe runs meticulousness and in a beautifully crafted way; the rising and setting of the sun, the changing of the seasons, and the delicately balanced order that is birth, growth and then decay. Uniformity in the laws of the universe point to the existence of a Creator and interestingly atheists that come to accept the message often start with a belief in a Creator God or Supreme Being. Convincing people that the Creator God is worthy of worship would be the next step.

In the final and third lesson we will look at delivering the message to specific people, particularly members of your own family.

INVITING NON-MUSLIMS TO THE RIGHT PATH: INVITING FAMILY, FRIENDS AND COLLEAGUES

Objectives:

·   To understand that we call to Islam by conveying the message but it is Allah who truly provides the guidance.

·   To understand the importance of perseverance and never giving up hope.

Arabic Terms:

·   Dawah - sometimes spelt Da'wah. It means to call or invite others to Islam.

·   Sunnah - The word Sunnah has several meanings depending on the area of study however the meaning is generally accepted to be, whatever was reported that the Prophet said, did, or approved.

· Du'a - supplication, prayer, asking Allah for something.

The aim of inviting people to the right path is to convey the message; we are not accountable if they do not convert. As mentioned earlier it is Allah that provides the guidance and the desire to accept Islam. Remember that whenever we intend to convey the message we must do so with wisdom, eloquent speech and in the most gracious manner. Arguments and heated discussions are not the best methods of dawah.

One who has accepted Islam must convey the message to those nearest and dearest to him. Once a person has tasted the sweetness of faith it becomes impossible not to desire that for all family members and friends. Calling family members must be a first priority but sometimes it can be the hardest work of all. Sometimes when you are the first member of your family to heed the message you plunge the other members of your family into a state of shock; especially if they do not mix with any Muslims in their daily lives.

Your family needs a little time to accept the reality. Make sure you have a supply of easy-to-read small books or pamphlets. If you live at home, you could leave them lying around, if not keep a supply in your bag or car. People often want to know this or that and sometimes you simply do not know the answer to all those questions. You are often just learning yourself so don't be tempted to make up an answer.

Perhaps you could look it up together remembering to always emphasis the Oneness of Allah, the Creator of all that exists.

Your family and close friends will be watching closely and this is when your behavior will play a big part. You have probably given up a lot of big things such as alcohol, parties, free mixing with the opposite gender, and pork and pork products. However, you have also added lots of little things; more kind acts, generosity, eagerness to be helpful, more gracious manners and a desire to establish strong unbreakable family ties. Showing kindness and observing high moral standards is possibly the best way to introduce someone to Islam. Good manners and courteous behavior are also a very good form of dawah. You are a role model for what Islam is all about.

Prophet Muhammad's behavior attracted others to Islam. His beloved wife Aisha called his character a living example of the Quran.[1] He was kind and courteous to everybody and even his enemies could not help but praise his noble character. This is the behavior we must endeavor to emulate and the people that will benefit the most are our family and close friends. A kind word, a smile, a gift, or help of any sort, will showcase the beauty of Islam.

Be particularly careful not to despair when you see your family or friends engaging in behavior that you now consider misconduct. Do not abandon them because of their ways. You can leave their company if they are drinking alcohol or acting in a non-Islamic manner - abandon the place, or the situation, not the person. Invite them to your house and to your events so they can see that fun and happiness can be found without alcohol or distasteful entertainment.

Conversations at your workplace are also a way to spread the message of Islam. Handing out pamphlets probably isn't going to win you any friends or influence people but your mannerisms and ways of dealing with people will. Remember however that your colleagues are likely to be as shocked as your family. If you have recently converted to Islam don't expect fanfare and congratulations but do expect curiosity. Again, don't give unqualified answers to things you are not sure about. The one thing you are sure about is the Oneness of Allah and His right to be worshipped.

Never give up hope. You may not see the people you love entering Islam and it can be a source of great disappointment. However, it is wise to remember that it is Allah that guides a person to the right path. Your role in that process might be as little as being a friendly face in an otherwise bleak day. Hope is something that Muslims have in abundance, so make small efforts and lots of du'a for the people you love and those around you.

Spreading the message and calling people to the right path is the work that was carried out by all of Allah's messengers. Each one called his own people to the One God, Allah. Prophet Muhammad however was sent to all of humankind; he gave the good news to the believers of immense reward in the Hereafter, and warning the unbelievers against a severe punishment. Prophet Muhammad expected all of those who follow in his footsteps to call others to the right path. He said, "If Allah guides one man through you, this will be better for you than possessing red camels.[2]"

"The Messenger of God is an excellent model for those of you who put your hope in God and the Last Day and remember Him often." (Quran 33:21)

In conclusion we find that if we follow the Quran and the Sunnah of Prophet Muhammad, we will present Islam in the best way possible and there is no better way of inviting others to the right path.

TRUST & RELIANCE IN ALLAH

Objectives:

· To understand the meaning of relying on Allah.

· To learn how to rely on Allah.

· To understand the benefit of reliance upon Allah.

Arabic Terms:

· Tawakkul – Reliance on Allah.

· Imaan - faith, belief or conviction.

· Al-Qadr - divine decree.

Meaning of Reliance Upon Allah
Trust in Allah "Reliance on Allah" is referred to in Arabic as tawakkul. The word literally means to place

one's affairs in the hands of another.

Allah has many Beautiful Names. One of Allah's personal Names associated with 'trust' is Al-Wakeel - the Disposer of Affairs. The Quran refers to Allah by Al-Wakeel fourteen times. For instance,

"And they said: 'Sufficient for us is Allah, and He is the best Disposer of Affairs'" (Quran 3: 173)

"Allah is sufficient as Disposer of Affairs." (Quran 4:81)

"He is the Disposer of all Affairs." (Quran 6:102)

Allah commands us to place our trust in Him: "(He is) the Lord of the East and the West. There is no true deity but He. Take Him, therefore, as Disposer of your Affairs." (Quran 73:9)

Likewise, Allah forbids us to place our reliance on His creation: "We gave Moses the Book, and made it a guide to the Children of Israel, (commanding): 'Take not other than Me as Disposer of (your) Affairs.'" (Quran 17:2)

Together, these two verses show us that reliance on Allah is an act of worship. Through our devoted trust and reliance, we express our monotheistic belief, and therefore these are things we should direct towards Allah alone.

How to Rely on Allah?
1. Do not confuse reliance with laziness

Tawakkul sometimes is mistaken for being laid back and thinking your problems will be solved without your intervention. Tawakkul should not be mistaken with giving up your efforts thinking that somehow your challenges will get resolved. Rather striving and working with the attitude that Allah will take care of your affairs and will help you in getting through your trials is part of you relying on Allah.

Reliance does not mean you do not work for provision, neglect education or not apply for a job, and miss an interview deadline. Allah has decreed that we must work and it is from His ways that He give people when they strive. Do not sit in your home and claim that your daily sustenance will come to you! Allah orders us to depend upon Him and to work at the same time. Thus, the act of striving for our sustenance is an act of physical worship while trusting in Allah is worship of the heart as Allah says, "So seek provision from Allah and worship Him (alone)." (Quran 29: 17)

Another way to truly understand trust is to look at what is Imaan. It is not just having faith in the heart, but it is a combination of faith and action. Similarly, reliance on Allah does not mean giving up on your own efforts. Rather it is to strive with the attitude that Allah will take care of your affairs and will help you get through the trials.

Remember when the Prophet asked a Bedouin, "Why don't you tie down your camel?" He replied, "I put my trust in Allah!" The Prophet then said, "Tie your camel first, then put your trust in Allah".[1]

2. Do not become arrogant

You should always plan and work based on what Allah has blessed you with. You should fully use those blessings by thanking Allah for them, without getting puffed up with arrogance about your personal strengths. All your strength and ability are from Allah and ultimately, it's the favor of Allah that will determine your success.

3. Accept Allah's Decisions

After your best efforts, accept whatever happens. You should believe that Allah, out of His wisdom, may decide to supersede all your plans for reasons that only He knows. Remind yourself that believing in al-Qadr (divine decree) is one of the pillars of your faith. Know that whatever will happen will happen and all you can do is your best.

4. Take all precautions

In the Quran Allah tells us the story of two prophets, Yaqub (Jacob) and his son Yusuf (Joseph). On one occasion, when sending his sons to Egypt, Yaqub instructs them to enter from different gates of the city to avoid suspicion, but Allah willed otherwise. The point is that Yaqub took all the measures he could to avoid any possible risk.

We must avoid a common pitfall. We tend to either rely on our efforts and forget trusting Allah or we think we are relying on Allah by not adopting any practical measures to solve our problems.

Benefits of Tawakkul

We need to apply tawakkul in our daily lives. One of the major benefits of tawakkul is that it can relieve us from unnecessary anxiety, worry, and resulting depression from the daily challenges. By believing that all our affairs are in Allah's hands and we can do only what is in our control, we leave the results to Allah and accept His decree whatever it may be. A sensible Muslim who understands tawakkul will not give up the effort, but will also not become overly elated with success or depressed by failure.

WHO IS A GOOD FRIEND? (PART 1 OF 2)

Objectives:

- To understand the role played by friends in our lives.

- To understand the importance of good Muslims friends and the influence of bad friends.

Arabic Terms:

- Shaytan- sometimes spelled Shaitan or Shaytaan.   It is the word used in Islam and the Arabic language to denote the devil or Satan, the personification of evil.

Much of our lives is spent in interaction with others. A structure of friendship can be represented by three concentric circles that can be described as very close, close, and not-so-close but still meaningful personal ties. An acquaintance will be in the 'not-so-close' category, someone you exchange small talk with as you go about your day, trade insights with online, or chat about sports. They will be people who cross our paths regularly like coworkers, classmates, and people we run into at the gym.

Close friendships, on the other hand, display strong support and affection. A close friend fills an indispensable role as a confidant, someone who listens and pays attention to you, is willing to help you, and has shared interests. A close friend is someone you trust and who shares a deeper level of understanding and communication with you; someone you can rely on, someone you can really connect with, and someone with whom you share a bond of trust and loyalty. No price tag on earth can be placed on their value and how much they mean to you. What makes a close friend different from a very close one? The answer is the level and extent you are able to confide deeply.

Importance of Developing Muslim Friendships
Muslim friends can provide tremendous emotional support and human contact that fulfill need for human companionship and reinforcement. The pull of healthy friendships can have an enormous effect on the quality of our lives. With growing numbers of people living alone, either by choice or circumstance, friendships occupy the emotional space that other people fill with spouses or significant others. Friends can link us to broader social networks and help enrich our lives.

There is no better way to judge ourselves than by

the company we keep. Even our Prophet did not go somewhere without any companions. He kept constant good company, even though he was aided by Allah Himself. The people who were by his side were guaranteed the highest place in Paradise. For example, Abu Bakr was his best friend even before Allah selected the Prophet to be His messenger. During his prophethood, he took two great journeys, one on earth and another to the heavens. When he migrated from the city of Mecca to Madina, he was accompanied by his closest companion, Abu Bakr. When he went from Jerusalem to the heavens, he was accompanied by Gabriel (Jibreel in Arabic), the greatest angel of Allah.

Our greatest journey is to our final destination – Paradise – and it is important that we take the best possible companions to accompany us in this journey. When we are faced by unrelenting temptations, our close friends are there to remind us of our purpose in this life and help us make better choices.

Many teens hang out with their friends more than with their close family members. Many go to school to be with their friends. We get together with friends for many reasons, like watching sports, playing games, or studying for an exam. Why not get together with friends to memorize the Quran or learn the basics of Islam, or study the life of the Prophet? It won't make you a scholar, but it will instill love for learning Islam. Having good Muslim friends will provide support and help we all need in school, college, and beyond.

The most important questions to ask yourself is,

'Do my friends, the people I hang out with, make me a better Muslim?'; 'Do they help me obey or disobey Allah?' Allah said in the Quran,

"Whoever obeys God and the Messenger will be among those He has blessed: the messengers, the truthful, those who bear witness to the truth, and the righteous - what excellent companions these are!" (Quran 4:69)

Our dear Prophet has reminded us,

"A person is with whom he loves." [1]

Those we love in this life will surround us in the Hereafter. A bad friend who pulls you down, takes you away from your purpose of creation, and pulls you towards what displeases Allah can be recognized by this verse of the Quran,

"And woe to me, if only I did not take him as a friend." (Quran 25:28)

If a friend's company was beneficial for us, then we will join them in Paradise; if they were detrimental to our faith, then may Allah protect us. The Day of Judgment is scary. All our securities, including friends and family, will leave us on that Day and we will be left with only our deeds to account for.

It boils down to, 'Are my friends preparing me for the Hereafter?' It is up to me to surround myself with good company otherwise Shaytan will pick me off. If we agree, follow and are pleased with bad friends, then we will likely inherit their habits, behaviors and even religious beliefs.

Everyone wants to belong to something or someone. When we constantly seek company with a certain type of people, we become more like them and act like them. It is natural. Gang members feel a sense of identity and pride as members of their crew. Many lose their lives or end up in prison before they realize it is too late. Most smokers start smoking because either their friends smoke or they encourage them to. It is almost always friends who influence such decisions.

Allah, the All-Wise also says: "Friends on that Day will be enemies one to another, except the pious." (Quran 43:67)

Friendship based on common core of faith will benefit and extend after this life. That is true friendship.

WHO IS A GOOD FRIEND? (PART 2 OF 2)

Objectives

- To learn about some places where one can meet Muslims to foster friendships.

- To understand some tips to engage in conversation.

- How to be a good friend?

Arabic Terms

- As-Salamu Alaikum - peace and blessings be on you.

- Eid - festival or celebration. Muslims celebrate two major religious holidays, known as Eid-ul-Fitr (which takes place after Ramadan) and Eid-ul-Adha (which occurs at the time of the Hajj).

·   Hijab – The word hijab holds several different meanings, including conceal, hide and screen. It commonly refers to a woman's headscarf and in broader terms to modest clothing and behavior.

·   Ramadan - The ninth month of the Islamic lunar calendar. It is the month in which the obligatory fasting has been prescribed.

·   Salam - The Islamic greeting such as 'As-Salamu Alaikum'.

Tip 1. Where to Meet Muslims?
Who Is a Good Friend21.jpgClose relationships will not happen overnight, but there are steps you can take to help you connect with other Muslims and make friends.

Attend the Friday prayer and some other prayers on a weekly basis. Even though it is time for worship, not socialization, you will get to know fellow Muslims who come regularly to the mosque and develop a special spiritual bond with them.

Take a class offered at your local mosque or Islamic center for new Muslims to meet others with common interests. Websites such as www.facebook.com and www.twitter.com can help you find local groups or start your own and connect with others who share similar interests.

Volunteering can be a great way to help others while also meeting new Muslims. Islamic centers are always looking for volunteers close to Eid and in Ramadan or other major events during the year. It provides an excellent opportunity to connect with other Muslims.

Attend community dinners at your mosque that are typically offered every month. Even if you are not used to the ethnic food or find it spicy, you will be able to meet new Muslims in a socially relaxed environment.

Attend Muslim community events, conferences, and lectures either in your locality or in neighboring cities or states where you can meet people with similar interests. You will meet new people, try new foods, and get a chance to buy clothes and books.

Tip 2. Learn to Engage in Conversation
Some people seem to instinctively know how to start a conversation with anyone in any place. If you're not one of these types, here are some easy ways to start a conversation with someone new:

Practice Islamic greeting and shake hands with confidence. Many people struggle with saying 'As-Salamu Alaikum.' You have to practice it so it becomes second nature in social gatherings. Remember, the Prophet said, "When two Muslims meet (give salam), and shake hands, they are forgiven their sins before they part (with each other)." (Abu Dawud)

Remark on the mosque and the Muslims

around you or the occasion. You could make some positive comments, such as: "I love the mosque," or "The food's great. Have you tried the chicken?".

Ask an open-ended question, one that requires more than just a yes or no answer. Ask a question that begins with one of the 5 W's or 1 H: who, where, when, what, why, or how. For example,

· "Who do you know here?"

· "Where do you normally go for Friday prayer?"

· "When did you move here?"

· "How is the food?"

Most people enjoy talking about themselves so asking a question is a good way to start a conversation.

Use a compliment. For example, "I really like your hijab, can I ask where you got it from?" or "Looks like you've done this before, can you show me?"

Listen effectively. People observed that when they were talking to Prophet Muhammad it was as if he was only interested in listening to them, he was fully focused. One of the keys to effective communication is to focus fully on the speaker and show interest in what's being said. Nod occasionally and smile at the person. The Prophet said, "Your smile in the face of your brothers is an act of charity"

(Tirmidhi).   Encourage the speaker to continue with small verbal cues like "yes" or "uh huh" and don't interrupt.

Tip 3. How to Be a Good Friend

Allah says in the Quran, "O mankind, We created you all from a single man and a single woman, and made you into races and tribes so that you may know one another." (Quran 49:13).   'They' don't just need to know us; we need to know 'them' too. We need to move out of our comfort zones.

Remember that making a friend is just the beginning of a journey into a relationship that will take time to deepen. Becoming friends is a process that requires time, effort, and a genuine interest in the other person. Follow some simple steps:

·   Be the friend that you would like to have. Treat your friend just as you want them to treat you. The Prophet advised, "None of you has faith until he loves for his brother what he loves for himself." (Saheeh Al-Bukhari, Saheeh Muslim)

·   Be a good listener. To develop a solid friendship with someone, be prepared to listen and support them just as you expect from them.

·   Invest in the friendship. No friendship will flourish without regular attention. Invite your new Muslim friend for dinner and plan activities with them.

·   Give your friend space. Do not be too needy

and be sure not to abuse your friend's generosity.

· Be forgiving. No one is perfect and every friend will make mistakes. Learn to forgive, it will deepen the bond of friendship between you. Allah describes the believers in the Noble Quran as those who constantly strive to have clean hearts, free from malice, hatred and spite. They supplicate for Allah's help to achieve this, "Our Lord, forgive us and those of our brothers who preceded us in faith, and do not place in our hearts any rancor against those who believe. Our Lord! You are indeed full of kindness, Most Merciful." (Quran 59:10)

PRIDE AND ARROGANCE

Objectives:

·   To understand the meaning of the Arabic word kibr and how it relates to arrogance and conceit.

·   To discover simple ways to banish pride and arrogance from our lives.

Arabic Terms:

·   Shaytan - sometimes spelled Shaitan or Shaytaan. It is the word used in Islam and the Arabic language to denote the devil or Satan, the personification of evil.

·   Kibr - arrogance, pride, haughtiness, conceit or condescension.

·   Dunya - this world, as opposed to the world of the Hereafter.

·   Sahabah - the plural form of "Sahabi," which translates to Companions.   A sahabi, as the word is commonly used today, is someone who saw Prophet Muhammad, believed in him and died as a Muslim.

·   Iblees – the Arabic name for Satan.

·   Risq – provision or sustenance. All aspects of a person's subsistence and livelihood fall under the definition of risq, including but not restricted to wealth and status.

·   Du'a - supplication, prayer, asking Allah for something.

Pride-and-Arrogance. The first entity to show pride and arrogance was Shaytan or as he is often called especially in the story of Adam, Iblees. He was filled with pride and arrogance because he thought that he was better than Adam. He felt superior.

"…then We told the angels, 'Prostrate to Adam', and they prostrated, except Iblees, he refused to be of those who prostrate. (Allah) said: 'What prevented you (O Iblees) from prostrating when I commanded you?' Iblees said: 'I am better than him (Adam), You created me from fire, and created him from clay'" (Quran 7:11-12)

That feeling of superiority is the root of all pride and arrogance. I am better than you. I make more money, my house is bigger, my intellect is greater, I have travelled more, my muscles are larger, I cook more delicious meals; the list goes on. One thing that all the things that we feel superior about have in common is that they are almost exclusively related to matters of the dunya. Love of the dunya and all its trappings actually push us further away from Paradise. Being, or appearing superior by dunya standards might just be more of a hindrance than a help. It is our God consciousness that makes a difference; being superior in that respect is the only superiority that counts.

You might make more money, but did you spend it to please Allah? You might make delicious meals but did you feed them to the poor? If you answer yes and you are proud of your accomplishments then this is not the pride and arrogance that translates to the Arabic word kibr (unhealthy and unnecessary pride and arrogance). Islam is not against innovation and achievement, it rewards and encourages excellence and success, and thus motivation, desire for reward and even desire for recognition are not the sins. The sin is in doing things with an incorrect intention. While achievement for the sake of Allah and to serve humanity is the correct intention, doing something for self-gain or self-love is an incorrect intention. Doing something to benefit your sense that the needs and desires of the world somehow revolve around you is kibr.

Kibr has the unintentional effect of making people dislike you, even fear you; it strips away respect. In addition, and of a far greater consequence is that it may deny you a place in Paradise. Prophet Muhammad often counselled the sahabah about the importance of humility. He said, "...Anyone who possesses half a mustard seed of kibr in his heart will not be granted admission to Paradise".[1]

"It will be said (to them), 'Enter the gates of Hell to abide herein, and (indeed) what an evil abode of the arrogant.'" (Quran 39:72)

Kibr puts our place in Paradise in jeopardy because it prevents us from acquiring the qualities of a believer. A prideful person is not capable of wanting for others what he wants for himself. Nor can he be humble or avoid envy. An arrogant person refuses to accept advice and is often unable to restrain his anger or wrath. A believer however, strives to remove these traits from his character. He is always mindful of his behavior.

Prophet Muhammad said that on the Day of Judgment Allah will not look at the person who drags his robe behind him out of pride. His close confidante Abu Bakr then responded, "Oh Messenger of Allah, one side of my robe slacks down but I am very cautious about it (i.e. I raise it)." Prophet Muhammad replied, "But you do not do that out of pride." [2] Once again we can see how prideful behavior, kibr, stems from the intention.

The remedy for kibr, and the means by which one can keep well away from pride and arrogance, is as simple as remembering who you are; just a human being, with a mother and father like everybody else. We all cry the same salty tears and bleed the same red blood. And we all have the same purpose in life; to worship Allah. We must also remind ourselves that all risq comes from Allah. One person might earn more money but it is Allah that allowed him to acquire the skills to do so. Another person might be more handsome or beautiful, but it is Allah that determined the quality of his or her genes. When we receive something that we perceive as a special blessing from Allah we should remind ourselves to be thankful and grateful. One step up from that would be to strive to use that blessing for the sake of Allah and to benefit humankind or this planet in some way.

Another remedy for kibr is to remember Allah; to keep Him in the forefront of our minds, if possible, at all times. Remember that Allah sees all, even what is in the hearts of each person. As Muslims we are blessed with a way or a system of remembering. We pray five times a day, we use specific words of remembrance, and we are encouraged to make du'a and remember Allah often. We use these methods to become close to Allah, to obey His commands and please Him. In doing so we protect our own hearts from the sins of desire and greed and the sins involved in feeling superior to those around us. This dunya is important because it is our ultimate test; not because it allows us to store up goods and chattels. We want to feel good about ourselves because we have achieved God consciousness and not because we take our risq and deceive ourselves into thinking we created it ourselves. Pride and arrogance should be banished from our lives and replaced with kindness and   compassion.

THE BENEFITS OF BEING A MUSLIM

Objectives:

·	To recognize the depth of meaning in all aspects of Islam.

·	To understand and appreciate how Islam reveals itself over time; according to a person's level of understanding and their growing needs.

Arabic Terms:

·	Dunya - this world, as opposed to the world of the Hereafter.

·	Akhirah - the Hereafter, the life after death.

·	Aayaat - (singular – ayah) the word aayaat can have many meanings. It is almost always used when talking about proofs from Allah. These include evidences, verses, lessons, signs, and revelations.

.   Hadith - (plural – ahadith) is a piece of information or a story.   In Islam it is a narrative record of the sayings and actions of Prophet Muhammad and his companions.

Benefits-of-Being-a-Muslim.

Having converted to the religion, the way of life, that is Islam, the new Muslim has clearly seen the benefits that would come from such a decision. These include being able to achieve tranquility and happiness even in the face of adversity and tribulation, understanding the meaning of life and establishing a relationship with Allah. However, after living Islam for some time these benefits come to have deeper dimensions and meanings not seen at first glance. Some of the benefits of being a Muslim are not fully revealed until a person has immersed himself in a lifestyle that is centered on pleasing the Creator. In this lesson we will take a closer look at the benefits that are revealed slowly over time.

1.   A deep and abiding relationship with Allah

Islam teaches that the purpose of life is to worship the Creator. Therefore, by converting to Islam and concentrating all one's efforts on pleasing Allah and following His guidance, believers are able to fortify the relationship that was forged in the act of conversion. The inner peace and tranquility that was acquired on that fateful day becomes a lasting happiness that cannot be maintained by following one's more base desires or accumulating material possessions. True contentment is now found only by worshiping and obeying the Creator.

"…Verily, in the remembrance of Allah do hearts find rest." (Quran 13:28)

2.   A pure concept of the nature of the Creator

The foundation of Islam is the worship of One God.   He is incomparable and unique thus the believer not only acknowledges this, he or she understands the depth of His complete perfection and greatness.   This understanding is inherent in all human beings and many people convert to Islam because the Islamic way of life encourages and strengthens this belief.   Over time the believer learns more about Allah and begins to understand His names and attributes and is able to integrate the nature of the creator into his everyday wants and needs.

"And (all) the Most Beautiful Names belong to Allah so call on Him by them…" (Quran7:180)

3.   A clear perspective on life

Islam encourages a believer to understand the events in his or her life in the context of the overall purpose of life.   The dunya was designed by our Creator to maximize our chances of living a blissful life in the akhirah.   Allah advises us to bear our trials and tribulations patiently.   This may at first be difficult but as one grows in understanding he or she can truly reconcile with the fact that everything that happens in this world happens by the permission of

Allah and whatever He does has wisdom and a reason behind it. No marriage ends, and no business fails without Allah's permission. Patience and gratitude for all our affairs is the formula for balanced life.

Prophet Muhammad, may the mercy and blessings of Allah be upon him, said: "How wonderful is the affair of the believer, for his affairs are all good. If something good happens to him, he is thankful for it and that is good for him. If something bad happens to him, he bears it with patience and that is also good for him." [1]

4.   An evidence-based faith

Islam is an evidence-based faith. It encourages people to open their hearts and minds to ponder the big questions such as life, love and the universe. God has provided signs in the dunya that point to Him and the wonder of His creation. The Quran encourages us to look at the visible signs and to think about them. This increases faith and certainty.

These signs are many and are visible and discernible to all. The earth, the sky, the sun, the moon, animals, rain, the miraculous workings of the human body, the nature of ecosystems... all these and much more point to a Creator. After converting to Islam these everyday miracles continue to be appreciated and add to one's faith and conviction.

We (Allah) have certainly sent down Signs that make things clear: and God guides whom He wills to the straight path." (Quran 24:46)

5.   Accountability and Justice

Just as each person is been given the capability to view and ponder the signs of Allah, they also have been given the free will to choose between right and wrong. Islam teaches that Allah is the Most Just and that on the Day of Judgement people will be held accountable for their deeds and questioned by Allah. One of the benefits that are not immediately discernible when a person converts to Islam is the number of ways Allah gives us to seek forgiveness of our sins or the number of chances, He gives a sincere believer. There are many aayaat (verses) and ahadith that tell us how to prepare ourselves for the final accounting and as we discover them the mercy and forgiveness of Allah becomes breathtaking.

Prophet Muhammad said: "Allah will bring the believer very close and privately ask him 'Do you know this sin? Do you know that sin?' The believer's reply will be, 'Yes Oh Lord,' until he is reminded about all of his sins, and he thinks he will perish. Then Allah will say 'I covered up your sins during your life, and I will forgive your sins today.' Then he will be given his book of good deeds." [2]

6.   A holistic way of life

Islam is a holistic way of life. Islam is a lifestyle not a religion practiced only on weekends or festive seasons. Life is organized in a spiritual and moral way, taking into account humankind's innate needs and desires. The tenets of Islam are derived from the

Quran and the authentic traditions of Prophet Muhammad and these two sources of revelation are a guide, or a manual for life. Islam teaches us to be concerned about the whole person. It teaches us to take into account our physical, emotional and spiritual needs and provides us with the best guidance in all matters.

By following the guidance and commandments of God, we are able to cope with trials and tribulations, and illness and injury, with patience and even gratitude. As a person spends more and more time living the way of life that is Islam the more, they are able to see how following the guidance of Islam steers us in a direction that satisfies all our needs.

SOME COMMON QUESTIONS BY RECENT CONVERTS

Objectives

·   To answer some of the questions frequently asked by new Muslims in order to dispel their early concerns.

Arabic Terms

·   Shahadah - Testimony of Faith.

·   Alhamdulillah – All praise and thanks is for Allah. By saying this we are thankful and we acknowledge that everything is from Allah.

·   Salat ul-Jumuah - Friday prayer.

(1)   I have recently accepted Islam; do I need to change my name?
No, you don't have to change your name unless its meaning is Islamically objectionable. The Prophet,

may the mercy and blessings of Allah be upon him, did not order everyone who accepted Islam to change their names. Since Arabic names generally have meanings, he did change names with offensive or religiously objectionable meanings. And if the name is not Islamically objectionable, then it is recommended to take a Muslim name but one does not have to.

Even if your first name does contradict Islamic principles and changing it in official documents would cause you much distress or harm, then it suffices to change it amongst family and acquaintances

If you do change your name, do not change the family name or your father's name, even if it be an impermissible name, but just your first name. Allah says in the Quran:

"Call them (adopted sons) by (the names of) their fathers, that is more just with Allah." (Quran 33:5)

(2)   I am uncircumcised male who just accepted Islam. Do I have to get circumcised?
Yes, it is mandatory to get circumcised after you accept Islam. However, if you cannot afford to get it done, or fear that it will harm you, then you can forgo or delay doing it. If you decide to go ahead with this meritorious act of worship, you need not go to extremes in hurrying to get it done. Make sure you find a good surgeon competent in circumcision before taking the step. The skin lesion takes about a week to completely heal. One of the benefits of having it done is that it makes it easier to clean

yourself, and maintain cleanliness, after passing urine or emitting semen, both of which your clothes and skin should be free from during prayer.

(3)   Do I have to say the Testimony of Faith (Shahadah) in front of people?
No. You do not have to utter the two testimonies:

Laa ilaaha ill-Allah, Muhammad-ur-Rasool-ullah,

…in front of people to be considered a Muslim in the sight of God. You can say it to yourself.

What is important is that:

(i)   you know the meaning of the Testimony of Faith

(ii) you actually utter the two testimonies verbally

(iii) your heart confirms it, you truly believe it, and intend to live by it to your best ability

The Messenger of Allah said:

"I testify that there is no god worthy of worship except Allah and that I am the Messenger of Allah. Every servant who meets Allah without doubting it will be admitted to Paradise." (Saheeh Muslim)

He also said,

"No one says 'La ilaha illa Allah' truthfully from their heart and dies upon it, but they will be protected from the Hell-Fire (i.e., they will be admitted into

Paradise)." (Saheeh al-Bukhari)

At the same time, it is perfectly fine, and to your advantage, to pronounce it publicly, like in a mosque, so people know you are a Muslim. In some countries one has to be registered as a Muslim, so, in the case of death, the person is given a Muslim burial. Also, it is good to get a letter at some point from your local Islamic center stating you are a Muslim. It may be useful when applying to go for the Hajj pilgrimage, or officially declaring a marriage in a Muslim country.

(4) Why is it necessary to say the two testimonies verbally?
A testimony is literally something which is given verbally and announced, not kept in the heart. Thus, the Testimony of Faith must be announced, and the Prophet himself would tell one who wished to accept Islam to pronounce it. Furthermore, it should be said in Arabic, as this statement is a specific prayer which is pronounced in Arabic.

(5) What are the common Islamic greetings I should know for social occasions?
The most important ones are two. When you meet a fellow Muslim, the one initiating the greeting says, 'As-Salamu 'Alai-kum.' The other responds, 'Wa 'Alai-kum us-salam.' Men shake hands with men and women shake hands with women. Men who are not mahram [1] to women should not shake their hands.

Also, a Muslim says, 'Alhamdulillah,' (All praise and thanks belong to Allah) on sneezing, and upon receiving good news or stating a pleasant state of affairs.

If one states that they will do something in the future, they should say, "In shaa-Allah (God-willing).

Also, if one praises something or someone, they should say, "Baarak-Allahu feeh (may Allah bless it), or Barak-Allahu feek (may Allah bless you)," respectively.

All these sayings have been taught by the Prophet of Islam.

(6) I have recently accepted Islam. I felt euphoric at the time, but sometimes I wonder if Islam is bringing me closer to God?

Without a doubt Islam brings a person closer to his Creator. God loves and wants you to be a Muslim. Rest assured of that. Islam links the human being to his true Lord through the belief in the oneness of God and through various acts of worship. The more one worships Allah, the more he draws near to Him. One will never be able to draw near to Allah except by first performing the obligatory deeds, as the Prophet said:

"God Almighty said, 'I have declared war on whoever shows enmity to a beloved slave of mine. My slave does not draw near to Me with anything I love more than by performing what I have obligated upon him, and he continues to draw near to Me with voluntary actions of worship until I love him. When I love him, I become his hearing with which he hears, his seeing with which he sees, his hand with which he strikes, and his foot with which he walks. If he were to ask Me for something, I would give it to him. If he were to ask Me for refuge, I would give him refuge.'" (Saheeh Muslim) [This Prophetic narration is not to be taken literally, rather what is meant is that the person will act according to that which pleases God. For example, he will not look at impermissible things, will only listen to that which is useful and beneficial such as listening to the Quran, Islamic lectures, etc.]

Stick the course. Be patient. Allow yourself time to grow as a Muslim. Learning is important and so is making good Muslim friends.

(7) I am new to Islam but I don't know any Muslims, and I am scared to approach a mosque, is there anyone available to help me?
You are welcome to go through the e-learning content of our website. You can also contact us via the support page and we will be happy to put you in contact with fellow Muslims close to you. We pray to God to bless you, and to make you steadfast in holding fast to the truth. God is the One who guides to the path of truth and light.

(8) Someone told me that Muslims cannot have any relationship with non-Muslims, is this true? All my family are non-Muslims and I don't want to cut ties with my family.
Beware of false information. What you were told is incorrect. Islam encourages us to be kind and generous to our relatives whether they are Muslim or

not. Especially, one's parents have great rights over us. You will find lessons where you will learn more about this.

(9) I heard that it is obligatory to attend Salat ul-Jumuah (Friday Prayer). What happens if my employer doesn't give me the time off to attend?

FATE OF NON-MUSLIMS

Objectives

· To learn about the Jews and Christians promised Paradise in the Quran.

· To learn the correct meaning of two frequently misunderstood verses of the Quran.

· To learn about the Islamic stand on the fate of non-Muslims.

Arabic Terms

· Tawheed – The Oneness and Uniqueness of Allah with respect to His Lordship, His Names and Attributes and in His right to be worshipped.

· Shirk – a word that implies ascribing partners to Allah, or ascribing divine attributes to other than Allah, or believing that the source of power, harm and blessings comes from another besides Allah.

- Kafir – (plural: kuffar) disbeliever.

The Jews and Christians Promised Paradise in Quran

The Jews and Christians promised Paradise in the Quran were Muslims who were true monotheists, practiced tawheed, believed in their prophets, did not commit shirk with Allah, but died before the prophethood of Muhammad, may the mercy and blessings of Allah be upon him. A frequently misunderstood verse of the Quran refers to them:

"Indeed, those who believe and those who are Jews and Christians, and Sabians (before Prophet Muhammad) – those (among them) who believed in Allah and the Last Day and did righteousness will have their reward with their Lord, on them shall be no fear, nor shall they grieve." (Quran 2:62)

The scholars of Islam agree this verse is not talking about those who believe Jesus is the son of God, or equate Jesus to God, or those who believe Allah is poor and they are rich, or who reject Prophet Muhammad, may the mercy and blessings of Allah be upon him. This verse is talking about the original followers of Moses and Jesus who believed in their prophet and worshipped Allah alone, but passed away before the coming of Prophet Muhammad. In fact, the Quran contains a whole chapter, Surah al-Buruj (Quran, 85), which speaks of the Christian martyrs before the advent of Prophet Muhammad in the story of 'the People of the Ditch.'

As for the verse:

"You will surely find the strongest among people in animosity to the believers to be the Jews and idolaters, and you will find the nearest in affection to the believers those who say: 'We are Christians.'" (Quran 5:82)

The rest of the verse explains the correct meaning. It is referring to Christians who entered Islam, believed in Prophet Muhammad, and were affected by the teachings of the Quran. Scholars of the Quran say this verse was revealed regarding Negus and his associates who entered Islam when a group of persecuted Muslims migrated to Ethiopia from Mecca. The Prophet offered the funeral prayer for Negus in absentia when he passed away. In the past and even today mostly Christians enter into Islam. That is why Christians are said to be closer in love to the Muslims.

"That is because among them are priests and monks, and they are not arrogant. And when they listen to what has been sent down to the Messenger, you see their eyes overflowing with tears, for they recognize the truth. They say: 'Our Lord! We believe; so, write us down among the witnesses. 'And why should we not believe in Allah and what has come to us of the truth? And we aspire that our Lord will admit us along with the righteous people.' Allah rewarded them for what they said with gardens under which rivers flow, they will abide therein forever. Such is the reward of good doers. But those who disbelieved and denied Our revelations they are the companions of Hellfire." (Quran 5:82-86)

The End of Non-Muslims
The Islamic stand on Jews, Christians, and other non-Muslims to be kuffar does not mean every non-Muslim is consigned to Hell. The People of the Book (Jews and Christians) in our times can be divided in two categories:

(I)   Those to whom the message of Islam has reached, who know Prophet Muhammad, on whom God's proof has been established, yet they have chosen not to believe in him. According to Muslims scholars, they are kuffar in this world and after they die, they will reside in Hell-Fire forever if they die on disbelief, on rejection. Apart from the verses of the Quran quoted previously, the Prophet Muhammad said:

"By Him in Whose hand is the life of Muhammad, he who amongst the community of Jews or Christians hears about me, but does not affirm his belief in that with which I have been sent and dies in this state (of disbelief), he shall be but one of the denizens of Hell-Fire." [1]

"When the Day of Resurrection comes a proclaimer will summon: Let every people follow what they used to worship. Then all who worshipped idols and stones besides Allah would fall into the Fire, till only the righteous and the sinners from those who worshipped Allah and others of the People of the Book are left. Then the Jews would be summoned, and it would be said to them: What did you worship?

They will say: We worshipped 'Uzair, son of Allah. It would be said to them: You tell a lie; Allah had never had a spouse or a son. What do you want now? They would say: We feel thirsty, O our Lord! Quench our thirst. They would be directed (to a certain direction) and asked: Why don't you go there to drink water? Then they would be pushed towards the Fire (and they would find to their great dismay that) it was but a mirage (and the raging flames of fire) would be consuming one another, and they would fall into the Fire. Then the Christians would be summoned and it would be said to them: What did you worship? They would say: We worshipped Jesus, son of God. It would be said to them: You tell a lie; Allah did not take for Himself either a spouse or a son. Then it would be said to them: What do you want? They would say: we are thirsty, O our Lord! Quench our thirst, and they will also suffer the same fate." [2]

(II)   The second category: those for whom the message of Islam did not reach, or it may have reached them but was distorted, or they did not hear about Prophet Muhammad. They will be tested on the Day of Judgment. Those who obey will be saved, those who disobey will be doomed.

As can be seen, the fate of the two will be different in life after death, but in this world, both are considered kuffar by agreement of Muslim jurists. What does it mean? First, it is obligatory to deliver the message of Islam to them. Second, Islam is the only true religion of all prophets with a universal plan of salvation; all other religions are false and unacceptable in the sight of Allah.   Third, the regulations for non-Muslims apply to them. For instance, regardless whether the message of Islam reached a non-Muslim or not, a Muslim woman cannot marry a Jewish or a Christian man. Furthermore, they may not be buried in a Muslim graveyard. Their funeral prayer cannot be offered by Muslims.

In conclusion, Islam is a universal religion. Its inclusiveness extends to the true followers of all prophets, including Moses, Jesus, and Muhammad. Yet, it is exclusive of those who distorted the pure teachings of the prophets, and who still choose to follow falsehood even after truth reaches them.

HOW TO DEAL WITH SADNESS AND WORRY (PART 1 OF 2): PATIENCE, GRATITUDE AND TRUST

Objective:

·   To utilize guidance from the Quran and the Sunnah of Prophet Muhammad to deal with the stresses of the 21st century.

Arabic terms:

·   Hajj – A pilgrimage to Mecca where the pilgrim performs a set of rituals. The Hajj is one of the five pillars of Islam, which every adult Muslim must undertake at least once in their life if they can afford it and are physically able.

·   Ramadan - The ninth month of the Islamic lunar calendar. It is the month in which the obligatory fasting has been prescribed.

·   Sabr - patience and it comes from a root word meaning to stop, detain, or refrain.

·   Shukr - thankfulness and gratitude, and to acknowledge the beneficence of Allah.

·   Sunnah - The word Sunnah has several meanings depending on the area of study however the meaning is generally accepted to be, whatever was reported that the Prophet said, did, or approved.

·   Tawakkul - to have complete faith or

confidence in something. In this case to trust Allah completely, demonstrated by the ability to accept our circumstances no matter what.

HowtoDealwithSadness1.jpgThe typical person in the developed world battles sadness and worry on a daily basis. At the same time, you will often hear similar people comment about how happy and content those who live in underdeveloped Muslim countries appear to be. Even facing extreme poverty, hunger and loss, they repeatedly accept their circumstances without complaint. Why do they not suffer from stress and anxiety? We could accept at face value, that because they face death on a daily basis, everything else pales in comparison or we could look a little deeper and wonder about their relationship with Allah.

In the 21st century religious beliefs do not give the same comfort we would have expected one hundred, fifty or even twenty years ago. We have everything available at our finger tips or at the touch of a button but technology does not hold our hand in the quiet of the night or soothe our fears when our heart beats erratically, and our souls are filled with unreasonable fears and anxiety. The religion of Islam is all about making and keeping a connection with God. Islam instructs us to deal with sadness and worry by turning to Allah with patience, gratitude and trust.

Great Islamic scholar of the 14th century CE, Ibnul Qayyim said that our happiness in this life and our salvation in the Hereafter depend on patience. He explained that having patience meant having the ability to refrain from complaining, or despairing, and also having the ability to control ourselves in times of sadness and worry.

Patience means accepting what is beyond our control. In times of sadness or worry, being able to surrender to the will of God is a relief beyond measure. This does not mean that we sit back and let life pass by without participating. It means striving to please God in all aspects of our lives and at all times bearing in mind that if things don't go the way we planned, or the way we wanted, we accept what Allah has decreed and continue to strive to please Him. Being patient is hard work; it does not always come naturally or easily, however Prophet Muhammad said, "Whoever tries to be patient then Allah will help him to be patient".

Patience and gratitude go hand in hand. Sabr and Shukr, are the Arabic words for patience and gratitude. Exercising patience becomes easier if we count our blessings and be grateful for them. We often forget that blessings from Allah include the air we breathe, the rain that falls from the sky, the sunshine on our faces or the shelter from rain and cold.

There are many ways to express gratitude but the easiest and most useful way is to obey Allah by fulfilling all our Islamic obligations. Simply by following the five pillars of Islam we express our gratefulness to Allah. When we bear witness that, there is no god worthy of worship but Allah and that Muhammad is His final Messenger we are being grateful for being blessed with Islam. When a believer prostrates before God in quiet, joyful prayer, we are expressing gratitude. During the fast of Ramadan, we become thankful for food and water by realizing that God provides our sustenance. If a believer is able to make the pilgrimage to the House of God in Mecca, it is indeed a cause for thankfulness. The Hajj journey can be long, difficult, and expensive.[1]

Practising Islam in the way Allah directed is an expression of patience and gratitude. If we accept and acknowledge as blessings the trials, triumphs, and tribulations of this life we open the way for the annihilation of all our worries and grief. All our experiences, from the highest highs to the lowest lows, are blessings from Allah. When we are overcome by sadness or worry, we must turn to Allah, strive to be patient and grateful and put our trust in Allah because Allah is the most trustworthy.

"The believers are only those who, when God is mentioned, feel a fear in their hearts and when His Verses (this Quran) are recited unto them, they (i.e., the Verses) increase their Faith; and they put their trust in their Lord Alone." (Quran 8:2)

This complete trust in Allah is called tawakkul. It means that we face life's trials, and triumphs knowing that whatever our circumstances Allah knows what is best for us. Our trust in Allah must be constant, in all situations, good, bad, easy, or difficult. Whatever happens in this world is with His permission. Allah provides sustenance and He is able to withdraw it.

Allah is the master of life and death; He is also the One who determines whether we are rich or poor, healthy or ill. If we are mindful that Allah has control over all things and that He ultimately wants us to live forever in Paradise, we can begin to leave our sadness and worry behind. If we face our fears and anxieties with complete trust in Allah, and if we show patience and gratitude with all our circumstances sadness and worry will disappear.

Prophet Muhammad said, "How wonderful is the affair of the believer, for his affair is all good, and this applies to no one except the believer. If something good happens to him, he gives thanks and that is good for him, and if something bad happens to him, he bears it with patience, and that is good for him." [2]

In the next lesson we will outline ways in which to become closer to Allah and thus begin to banish worry and sadness from our lives.

HOW TO DEAL WITH SADNESS AND WORRY (PART 2 OF 2): ESTABLISH A RELATIONSHIP WITH ALLAH

Objective:

·   To suggest three ways of becoming closer to Allah.

Arabic terms:

·   Sabr - patience and it comes from a root word meaning to stop, detain, or refrain.

·   Shukr - thankfulness and gratitude, and to acknowledge the beneficence of Allah.

·   Du'a - supplication, prayer, asking Allah for something.

In order to live our lives with complete trust in Allah it is necessary to build a relationship with our Creator. In order to deal with the sadness and worry that seems to be a part of everyday life in the developed world we need to rely on Allah. If we put our faith and trust in Him, and bear the trials and tribulations that come our way with sabr and shukr, our outlook on life changes. Of course, we cannot expect to be worry free because facing obstacles is part of the human condition. However, facing problems armed with trust in Allah and contentment with His decree for us makes life easier and happier.

You cannot completely trust someone without knowing them well and the same can be said with trusting Allah. Before we submit ourselves to the will of Allah, we must know who it is we are submitting to. There are a number of ways that a person can establish a relationship with Allah. In addition, staying close to Allah will help us combat the inevitable pains and sorrows that form part of being alive. We will examine just three of the numerous ways a person can reach out to Allah and cope in times of sorrow and stress.

Calling on Allah by His Most Beautiful Names
Muslims are encouraged to remember Allah and be grateful to Him at all times, however this can be especially beneficial if one is lost in the depths of despair or even just feeling mildly stressed by the day or the week. We are encouraged to know Allah's Beautiful Names and thus, we are able to know our Creator and are able to call on Him by the Names that are indicative of our needs.

Prophet Muhammad encouraged us to call on Allah by all of His Most Beautiful Names. In his own supplications, he is known to have said, "Oh Allah, I ask you by every name that You have named yourself, or that You have revealed in Your book, or that You have taught any of Your creation, or that You have kept hidden in the unseen knowledge with

Yourself".[1]

"Allah! (None has the right to be worshipped but He)! To Him belong the Best Names." (Quran 20:8)

"And (all) the Most Beautiful Names belong to Allah, so call on Him by them ..." (Quran 7:180)

Contemplating the Names of Allah can bring great relief. It makes us realize His greatness and increases our faith. It can also help us focus on being calm and patient. It is important to understand that although the believer is encouraged not to thrash about in grief and anguish or to complain about the stresses and problems, he is encouraged to turn to Allah, supplicate to Him and to ask Him for relief. Using the names of Allah that correspond with the need is also a commendable and calming act.

Making dua at every opportunity
If a person is feeling distressed it is important to remember that Allah is close by and one effective way to reach Him is by making du'a. When one calls upon the Most Merciful, He (Allah) will respond. "And when My slaves ask you concerning Me, then (answer them), I am indeed near (to them by My Knowledge). I respond to the invocations of the supplicant when he calls on Me. So let them obey Me and believe in Me, so that they may be led aright." (Quran 2:186)

Prophet Mohammad taught his followers a dua specifically for those of us feeling sorrowful and distressed.

"There is no-one who is afflicted by distress and grief, and says: Allaahumma inni 'abduka ibnu 'abdika ibnu amatika naasiyati bi yadika, maadhin fiyya hukmuka, 'adlun fiyya qadaa-uka. Asaluka bi kulli ismin huwa laka sammayta bihi nafsaka aw anzaltahu fi kitaabika aw 'allamtahu ahadan min khalqika aw ista-tharta bihi fi 'ilmil-ghaybi 'indaka, 'an taj-'alal-Qur-aana rabee'a qalbi wa noor sadri wa jalaa huzni wa dhahaaba hammi (O Allah, I am Your slave, son of Your male slave, son of Your female servant; my forelock is in Your hand, Your command over me is forever executed and Your decree over me is just. I ask You by every name belonging to You which You have named Yourself with, or revealed in Your Book, or You taught to any of Your creation, or You have preserved in the knowledge of the Unseen with You, that You make the Quran the life of my heart and the light of my chest, the banisher of my sadness and the reliever of my distress), but Allah will take away his distress and grief, and replace it with joy." He was asked: "O Messenger of Allah, should we learn this?" He said: "Of course; everyone who hears it should learn it." [2]

Du'a increases faith, gives hope and relief to the distressed and saves the supplicant from despair and isolation. Making sincere du'a is indeed a weapon that can battle even the most serious stress and sorrow. There are countless occasions when the prophets and our righteous predecessors have made du'a and Allah's response was to save them from what was certain danger, calamity or pain.

Understanding the reality of the life of this world
Often misfortune, pain, and suffering come about because of our own actions.   We choose to commit sin, but Allah purifies us through loss of wealth, health or the things we love.   Sometimes suffering now, in this world compensates for the suffering in the next life; sometimes all that pain and distress means that we will attain a higher station in Paradise.

Allah knows the ultimate wisdom behind why good things happen to bad people, or why bad things happen to good people. In general, whatever causes us to turn to Allah is good.   In times of crisis people are drawn closer to Allah.   Allah is the Provider and He is the Most Generous.   He wants to reward us with life everlasting and if pain and suffering can bring us closer to Paradise, then ill health and injuries are a blessing.   Prophet Muhammad said, "If Allah wants to do good to somebody, He afflicts him with trials." [3]

DEALING WITH DOUBTS

Objectives

·   To understand that doubts in one's faith are a natural human occurrence.

To acquire the tools with which to banish these doubts.

Arabic Terms

·   Shaytan - sometimes spelled Shaitan or Shaytaan. It is the word used in Islam and the Arabic language to denote the devil or Satan, the personification of evil.

·   Sunnah - The word Sunnah has several meanings depending on the area of study however the meaning is generally accepted to be, whatever was reported that the Prophet said, did, or approved.

·   Jinn – A creation of Allah that was created before humankind from smokeless flame. They are referred to at times as spirit beings, banshees, poltergeists, phantoms and so forth.

·   Ummah - Refers to the whole Muslim community, irrespective of color, race, language or nationality.

Dealing With Doubts

Doubts about what we believe and why we believe it are natural. In fact, it is often those doubts that cause people to embrace Islam. A doubt about the validity of their belief systems often sends people on a search for something they can understand and believe in. Having doubts about your chosen religion or aspects of that religion may happen but the difference is that

Islam allows us to be both forewarned and forearmed to deal with doubts. Islam is often described as 'informed knowledge' rather than blind faith, therefore when doubts arise, we are able to deal with them. Doubts are a disease that can cause great damage to our spiritual health if they are left to fester rather than be confronted for what they are – tricks and illusions thrown at us like arrows from the bow of Shaytan.

Shaytan is humankind's sworn enemy. Just as he is able to whisper evil thoughts into our hearts, he is also able to fill our minds with doubts, doubts that are designed to cause disquiet and confusion. Sometimes a person is unable to distinguish between what is planted by Shaytan and what we think of our own volition. On other occasions the thoughts are of such a frightening nature that we are afraid to repeat them or examine them in case they condemn us or reveal us to be hypocritical or away from Islam. One should completely ignore such thoughts and doubts and not ponder over them and seek refuge from Shaytan in Allah. Say "a'udhu billahi minash-shaytaanir-rajeem" (I seek refuge in Allah from the accursed Shaytan) and ask for forgiveness.

From the traditions of Prophet Muhammad, may the

mercy and blessings of Allah be upon him, we are told that if one is afflicted by doubt in his faith he should seek refuge in Allah, renounce what is causing the doubt and say, "Aamantu billaahi wa rusulihi", which means, I believe in Allah and His messenger.[1]

There is no protection from the destruction that can be inflicted by these doubts, except by turning to Allah. So, when doubts trouble your heart, mind or soul turn to Allah and find comfort in obedience to Him and in seeking to please Him. In the Sunnah of Prophet Muhammad, we find a beautiful Prophetic narration in which Allah speaks directly to the believers. Thus, when doubts arise seek guidance from Allah alone, recognize our complete and utter dependence upon His mercy and face down those doubts armed with knowledge and good deeds.

"'O My slaves, I have forbidden oppression for Myself and have made it forbidden amongst you, so do not oppress one another. O My slaves, all of you are astray except for those I have guided, so seek guidance from Me and I shall guide you. O My slaves, all of you are hungry except for those I have fed, so seek food of Me and I shall feed you. O My slaves, all of you are naked except for those I have clothed, so seek clothing from Me and I shall clothe you. O My slaves, you sin by night and by day, and I forgive all sins, so seek forgiveness from Me and I shall forgive you. O My slaves, you will not harm Me nor will you benefit Me. O My slaves, were the first of you and the last of you, the human of you and the jinn of you to be as pious as the most pious heart of any one man of you, that would not increase My kingdom in anything. O My slaves, were the first of you and the last of you, the human of you and the jinn of you to be as wicked as the most wicked heart of any one man of you, that would not decrease My kingdom in anything. O My slaves, were the first of you and the last of you, the human of you and the jinn of you to rise up in one place and make a request of Me, and were I to give everyone what he requested, that would not decrease what I have, any more than a needle decreases the sea if put into it. O My slaves, it is but your deeds that I reckon up for you and then recompense you for, so let him who finds good praise Allah and let him who finds other than that blame no one but himself.'" [2]

The thing that Shaytan likes most is being able to lead one who has found the truth away from his chosen path. He tries his best to instill doubts and he is best able to do that by filling up the spaces in a person's mind that are not already filled with authentic knowledge. Thus, it is important to continue to seek knowledge from the cradle to the grave. Or, in other words from the time you first began to ponder the validity of Islam until the time you stand face to face with the angel of death.

Due to our limited knowledge, we may not understand certain statements or the wisdom in certain injunctions and this may lead to doubts. In a situation such as this, one should reaffirm their faith by looking at the fundamentals of Islam; since it is accepted intellectually, the few things that one may feel doubtful in, shouldn't stand as a problem, for we believe Allah is All-powerful, All-wise!

As Muslims, we believe firmly that all things have a sure wisdom behind their creation; at times, we understand the wisdom, and at other times we do not. Our ignorance in terms of the reason behind something doesn't negate the fact that there is a reason. It's only on account of our own shortcomings that we are unable to comprehend certain matters. This has been proven over the course of our natural history; many things in the past were relatively unknown, mysterious, and thought of as being something an oddity, but as science progressed, the wisdom behind those matters has become clear. Take the appendix as an example, a few years ago, it was only thought of as a useless body organ, but now as science has progressed, the wisdom behind its existence has become clear!

In a nutshell, we have not been told the reason and wisdom of everything. And if one has doubts about the fundamentals of Islam then one should look at the proofs of Islam in greater detail so as to strengthen their faith.

In this day and age, we are faced with unbelievable access to knowledge from all over the world and sadly this includes many sites and sources that try to revile Islam by twisting facts, quoting textual passages out of context, quoting weak and fabricated traditions from the Sunnah or simply by forging lies against Islam. It is important that you learn about Islam from reliable sources.

Even the companions of Prophet Muhammad were troubled with negative thoughts and there is a wealth of evidence in the Sunnah that explains the normality of these experiences.

"Allah has forgiven for my Ummah that which is

whispered to them and which crosses their minds, so long as they do not act upon it or speak of it." [3]

It was narrated that Abu Hurayrah (may Allah be pleased with him) said: "Some of the companions of the Messenger of Allah, came to the Prophet and said to him, 'We find in ourselves thoughts that are too terrible to speak of.' He said, 'Are you really suffering from that?' They said, 'Yes.' He said, 'That is a clear sign of faith.'" [4]

Thus, if a person experiencing doubts feels bad and distressed because of this, then he should not be overly worried or frightened, as Prophet Muhammad said, these thoughts are "signs of faith"! Islamic scholars have explained that just as a thief only strikes at a place where he knows that there is wealth and that the defenses of that location are weak, similarly Shaytan only strikes and puts doubts into hearts that contain the wealth of true faith.

God gives us a simple and clear method in the Quran in terms of dealing with doubts. He says:

"Ask the people of knowledge if you do not know."

(21:7)

The presence of doubts indicates a form of ignorance that is only removed by knowledge. The more one educates themselves and strengthens their faith, the stronger they will become in repelling nagging doubts.

DRUGS, ALCOHOL, & GAMBLING (PART 1 OF 2)

Objectives

- Recognize the effect of drinking alcohol on the

human mind and body.

·   Learn the verses of the Quran and hadith of Prophet Muhammad on alcohol and drugs.

·   Learn the Islamic ruling on alcohol and drugs.

Arabic Terms

·   Hadith - (plural – ahadith) is a piece of information or a story. In Islam it is a narrative record of the sayings and actions of Prophet Muhammad and his companions.

·   Khamr – Any drink, drug, or substance that causes intoxication.

·   Salah - the Arabic word to denote a direct connection between the believer and Allah. More specifically, in Islam it refers to the formal five daily prayers and is the most important form of worship.

- Surah - chapter of the Quran.

Drugs and Alcohol

Alcohol is part of the Western culture—it is used in celebrations and socialization, and it enhances religious ceremonies. Most Americans recognize that drinking too much can lead to accidents and dependence. But that's only part of the story. In addition to these serious problems, alcohol abuse can damage organs, weaken the immune system, and contribute to cancers. Furthermore, drinking kills 1,400 college students each year in the US [1] and contributes to 100,000 deaths annually, making it the third leading cause of mortality in the US, after tobacco and diet/activity.[2] During 2007 a total of 38,371 drug-induced deaths occurred in the US.[3]

As an example of what it does to the brain, The National Institute on Alcohol Abuse and Alcoholism states,

"Difficulty walking, blurred vision, slurred speech, slowed reaction times, impaired memory: Clearly, alcohol affects the brain. Some of these impairments are detectable after only one or two drinks and quickly resolve when drinking stops. On the other hand, a person who drinks heavily over a long period of time may have brain deficits that persist well after he or she achieves sobriety. Exactly how alcohol affects the brain and the likelihood of reversing the impact of heavy drinking on the brain remain hot topics in alcohol research today.

We do know that heavy drinking may have extensive and far–reaching effects on the brain, ranging from simple "slips" in memory to permanent and debilitating conditions that require lifetime custodial care. And even moderate drinking leads to short–term impairment, as shown by extensive research on the impact of drinking on driving." [4]

Drug and alcohol dependence often go hand in hand. Research shows that people who are dependent on alcohol are more likely to use drugs, and people with drug dependence are much more likely to drink alcohol.[5]

Islam, our beautiful religion, provides us guidance about drugs and alcohol. Islam views drugs and alcohol in the category of prohibited and forbidden. Any amount of drugs or alcohol is forbidden to use. Taking even a little wine for social drinking is totally forbidden. Once developed, the habit of drinking in small amounts soon develops into an addiction.

Allah has forbidden drugs and drinks in the Quran:

O you who have believed, indeed, intoxicants, gambling, [sacrificing on] stone alters [to other than Allah], and divining arrows are but defilement from the work of Satan, so avoid it that you may be successful. Satan only wants to cause between your animosity and hatred through intoxicants and gambling and to avert you from the remembrance of Allah and from prayer. So, will you not desist? (Quran 5:90-91)

When these verses were revealed to the Prophet, an announcement was made that those who have alcohol were forbidden to drink or sell it. All stocks were ordered to be destroyed. Thereafter, alcohol was drained in the streets of the city of Madina.

One person asked if alcohol can be used as medicine. The Prophet said, "It is not a medicine, it is a disease." [7]

The Prophet prohibited alcohol in strong words. He said:

"Truly, Allah has cursed khamr, the one who produces it, the one for whom it is made, the one who consumes it, and the one who serves it, the one who carries it, the one for whom it is carried, the one who sells it, the one who earns from the sale of it, the one who buys it, and the one for whom it is bought." (Tirmidhi, Ibn Majah)

The Arabs before Islam were fond of alcohol and drinking parties. They had one hundred names for alcohol in their language. To eradicate this evil, Allah adopted a step-wise approach to prohibit it.

In the first stage, Allah expressed disapproval of drinking and gambling (Surah al-Baqarah 2:219). The second phase forbade people from praying in state of drunkenness (Surah an-Nisa 4:43). In the third and final phase, the prohibition was absolute (Surah al-Maidah 5:90-91).

Any drink, drug, powder, or substance that intoxicates is

forbidden.   Allah's Prophet said, "Every intoxicant is khamr, and every khamr is forbidden." (Saheeh Muslim)

He also said, 'What intoxicates in a large quantity is forbidden even in a small quantity.' (Abu Dawood and Tirmidhi)

What this means is that a sip of any alcoholic drink or a small quantity of a drug is also forbidden.

DRUGS, ALCOHOL, & GAMBLING (PART 2 OF 2)

Objectives

·   Recognize the widespread forms of gambling in modern society.

·   Learn the Islamic ruling on gambling and its types.

·   Learn six ways to deal with the vices of alcohol, drugs, and gambling.

Arabic Terms

·   Du'a - supplication, prayer, asking Allah for something.

·   Sunnah - The word Sunnah has several meanings depending on the area of study however the meaning is generally accepted to be, whatever was reported that the Prophet said, did, or approved.

Gambling

Gambling discourages honest labor and encourages greed, materialism and discontent. It encourages "get rich quick" thinking and reckless investment of God-given resources.

"Gambling addiction" is a recognized mental health problem![1] Betting on sports, buying lotto tickets, playing poker, slot machines, or roulette are only a few of the activities in which compulsive gamblers engage. While many prefer gambling in a casino, the rate of online gambling addiction is on the rise.

Islam forbids gambling. The prohibition is based on the Quran and the Sunnah of the Prophet. In the Quran, we read:

"O you who believe! Intoxicants and gambling, (dedication of) stones and (divination by) arrows, are an abomination of Satan's handwork: Abstain from such (abomination), that you may prosper. Satan's plan is (but) to excite enmity and hatred between you with intoxicants and gambling, and hinder you from the remembrance of Allah, and from prayer. Will you not then abstain?" (Surah al-Maidah 90-91)

The Messenger of Allah emphasized the prohibition of gambling to such an extent that even considering to take part in gambling was regarded to be blameworthy. The Messenger of Allah said: "Whosoever says to another: 'come lets gamble' should give in charity (as a form of expiation for intending to gamble)." (Saheeh Al-Bukhari)

We can say that gambling is an activity in which the players voluntarily transfer money or something of value among themselves, but this transaction is conditional to the outcome of a future event that is uncertain.

Basically, there are two fundamental formations of gambling:

1) The first form of gambling is when no party is obliged to pay any amount for certain; rather, the payment of each party is dependent upon an uncertain event in the future. In this case, the gambler does not stake his money initially, rather the money is put at stake by promising to pay later.

For example, A and B compete in a race, with the promise of the loser paying the winner $100. In this example, there is no certainty of payment from any one party; rather the payment is contingent from both sides on winning and losing.

Also included in this category is the betting that takes place in horse-racing and various other sports. For example, A says to B that if team X wins the match, I will pay you $100, but if team X loses, you will have to pay me $100.

2) The second form of gambling is where payment is certain from one side, and uncertain from the other. The one paying for certain is actually staking his wealth, in that it may bring more wealth or it may be lost totally. This is probably the most widespread type of gambling and has many different forms.

Also included are the various types of lotteries, raffles, and sweepstakes, where one has to pay to be included in the draw, whether this payment is in the form of entrance-fees, purchasing of tickets or any other form. The reason is that the total accumulated cash will be distributed among those whose names emerge in the draw as the prize-winners, which is clear gambling. If one's name does not emerge in the prize draw, one will be losing wealth without anything in return.

Treatment Plan

1.   Proper Upbringing

A healthy family provides the stability children need and when it instills in children the love and fear of Allah, it becomes a strong deterrent against following desires. The most effective manner to parent is to provide good role models to one's children. Not only words, but action is also required from parents.

2.   Repent & Seek Forgiveness

A believer immediately seeks forgiveness after committing a sin and feels ashamed for having disobeyed Allah. Therefore, any Muslim who is involved in drug abuse, alcoholism, or gambling, must know that Allah is there to help him and forgive him his sins. He must go to Allah with a repentant heart. The Prophet of Mercy said, "The one who repents from sin is like the one who has not committed any sin." (Ibn Majah)

However, repentance should be totally sincere. A person has to feel ashamed and guilty for doing the sin. He should also resolve to stay away from that sin in future. He should make amends to compensate for that sin.

3.   Keep Good Company

Keeping good company is part of the treatment as well as prevention. Without it, the treatment is incomplete. A person should make every effort to develop good relations. Being surrounded by good, pious people cannot be over emphasized. When a person is deprived of sincere friends, he has no one to remind or advise him when he is feeling sad or lonely. Many people fall into the vices of drugs, alcohol, and gambling through exposure to bad company. Live close to the mosque and spend time in it, change neighborhoods, move out of the city, do whatever it takes.

4.   Occupy Your Time

When a person with free time fails to utilize it in obedience of Allah, he will likely use it to disobey Allah. Most addicts complain of boredom! Free time should be seen and utilized as an opportunity to please Allah and gain His rewards in the Hereafter. The Prophet said "There are two blessings of which many people are deprived: health and free time." (Saheeh Al-Bukhari)

Use your time to learn the Quran, learn Arabic, learn about Islam, then spread it. Use your free time to develop skills, get training for a job, or education.

5.   Consult a Rehab Center

Get into a rehab program and get all the help you need.

6.   Du'a (Supplication)

Du'a in itself is an effective treatment. In du'a one implores the All-Powerful by Whose command everything occurs. When one combines du'a with other efforts, Allah most certainly helps and protects His servants.

GOOD HABITS FOR NEW MUSLIMS TO DEVELOP

Objective:

· To provide new Muslims with some guidelines to learn more about Islam, and to gain insight into some of the beneficial practices that make following Islam easy.

Arabic Terms:

· Insha'Allah – God willing, if God wills it to be so. It is a reminder and acknowledgment that nothing happens except by the will of Allah.

· Alhamdulillah – All praise and thanks is for Allah. By saying this we are thankful and we acknowledge that everything is from Allah.

· SubhanAllah – How Perfect is Allah, far removed is Allah from every imperfection.

· Allahu Akbar – Allah is the Greatest.

After a person has accepted Islam as their religion, they will come to realize that Islam is more than just a religion - it is way of life. Worship is not reserved for special days or special ceremonies; it is a part of our living and our dying, our working and our play, our rest and our study. In short Islam is something that we live with all our actions, thoughts and deeds. Developing good habits to assist us in our everyday lives as a worshipper of the One God is easy. Below you will find a few guidelines to get you started. They are habits that should Insha'Allah become as familiar as breathing.

1.   Dedicate some part of everyday to reading a translation of the Quran.

2.   Pay strict attention to learning how to pray. Try to improve your prayers until you are satisfied that you are praying in the correct manner. Sometimes this takes longer than you might expect, so do not be discouraged.

3.   Try to learn some words of remembrance. These can be said at any time of the day or night. If

you feel you do not know enough of the prayer ritual but want to spend longer connected to Allah then they can even be repeated at the end of your prayer. Learn to say: SubhanAllah, Alhamdulillah and Allahu Akbar.

"Therefore, remember Me (by praying, glorifying), I will remember you, and be grateful to Me (for My countless Favors on you) and never be ungrateful to Me." (Quran 2:152)

4.	Give some form of charity every day. Remember that in Islam giving charity can be as simple as smiling and brightening a person's day.

The Prophet Muhammad said, "Every Muslim has to give in charity." The people then asked: "(But what) if someone has nothing to give, what should he do?" The Prophet replied: "He should work with his hands and benefit himself and also give in charity (from what he earns)." The people further asked: "If he cannot find even that?" He replied: "He should help the needy who appeal for help." Then the people asked: "If he cannot do (even) that?" The Prophet said finally: "Then he should perform good deeds and keep away from evil deeds, and that will be regarded as charity." [1]

"Every act of kindness is charity." [2]

5. Avoid wasting your free time. You will discover that there 1001 things to do that are beneficial. Time wasted on video games and idly surfing the internet can be better spent. Once you understand that every single thing can be a way of worshipping Allah then playing video games for hours on end does not seem to be a very wise way to spend time. Having said this however we now come to the next point.

6. Avoid going to extremes. It may be tempting to fast every day or read all of the Quran in one sitting but Prophet Muhammad warned us against going to extremes. Therefore, in a 24-hour day there is time to play and time to learn.

"Religion is very easy and whoever overburdens himself in his religion will not be able to continue in that way. So, you should not be extremists..." [3]

7.   Islam is a holistic religion; it requires us to pay attention to our spiritual, physical and mental health. Therefore, acquire habits that keep you healthy and add to your Islamic character. Getting enough sleep at night allows you to rise early to pray. Eating the right foods in the right quantities keeps you energetic rather than lazy; this allows you to worship without hardship.

8.   Try to make friends in the Muslim community. Staying in the company of people who worship Allah in the correct manner is a source of fun and benefit. The best friends are those who talk about Islam more than the latest fashions. Good friends remind each other of their Islamic obligations, such as praying on time or the importance of helping others.

9.   Try to read about the life and times of Prophet Muhammad. There are many good books in all languages that teach about the noble life of Allah's final messenger. As Muslims we should love the Prophet but how do we love someone we do not know.

"Indeed in the Messenger of Allah you have a good example to follow for him who hopes in (the Meeting with) Allah and the Last Day and remembers Allah much." (Quran 33:21)

10. Acquire virtuous manners and morals. Learn about and try to emulate the morals and manners of the Prophet Muhammad, those who lived around him and all of our righteous predecessors, including all the Prophets of Allah. Allah expects us to behave in the best manner, if we fail sometimes then we should seek forgiveness and try to do better.

Our religion is easy. It is one small step at a time. Slowly but surely acquire the habits that will make life in this world better and a better life in the hereafter secure.